SILVER *FOXES*

SILVER
FOXES

OLDER, WISER AND A DAMN SIGHT *SEXIER*

DAWN PORTER

2 4 6 8 10 9 7 5 3 1

Published in 2011 by Virgin Books, an imprint of Ebury Publishing
A Random House Group Company

www.randomhouse.co.uk

Address for companies within The Random House Group Limited can be found at
www.randomhouse.co.uk/offices.htm

The Random House Group Limited Reg. No. 954009

A CIP catalogue record for this book is available from the British Library

ISBN 9780753539934

The Random House Group Limited supports the Forest Stewardship Council® (FSC®),
the leading international forest certification organisation. All our titles that are printed on
Greenpeace approved FSC® certified paper carry the FSC® logo. Our paper
procurement policy can be found at **www.randomhouse.co.uk/environment**

Design and typesetting Smith & Gilmour
Printed and bound in China by Toppan Printing Co., (SZ) Ltd

To buy books by your favourite authors and register for offers visit
www.randomhouse.co.uk

FOREWORD

It's fair to say that, for the most part, old age isn't something we look forward to: wrinkles, aching joints and Stannah stair lifts all paint a picture of the latter days of life that make us do everything we can to fight it off. But there is one aspect of getting older that makes it more of a delicious benefit than an irritating fact of life. It's a feature that leaves women feeling happier about time going by than anything else – a visual treat that only maturity can bring. It offers a generous helping of eye candy that steals the light from the pitfalls of growing old. It makes us swoon, it makes us giddy, and it turns us on in a simply inexplicable way. I am, of course, talking about that delicious moment when a man goes grey.

Most commonly known as the Silver Fox, this hot and virile breed of gentleman has everything – including age – on his side. For most women, a head of silver hair on a man is irresistible, but why? Is it because it gives off a sense of wisdom and experience? Yeah, there's that, I guess, but the real reason is as simple as this – it's just damn sexy.

Don't be fooled, this isn't just a book for the over 50s. Some men's tresses have turned them into foxes way before they've even hit 40. Lucky them! And here they are for us to gawp at as openly as we please. But this book isn't about age, it's about beauty, and it shows that, no matter how old the man with a head of silver hair may be, he is sure to be looking foxier than ever.

This is a collection of some of the sexiest Silver Foxes of all time. We have everyone from George Lamb to George Clooney, and each of them deserves their spot in this gallery of grey gorgeousness that is sure to have all the ladies fighting for hair – sorry, air, as we set aside the negative side effects of old age, and wish that whoever invented Just for Men had never got out of bed that day.

Dawn Porter, June 2011

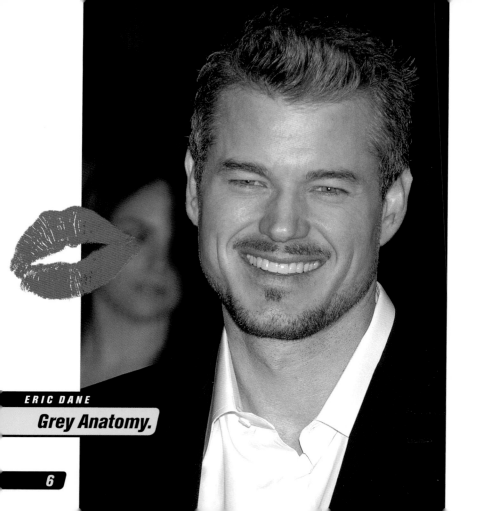

ERIC DANE
Grey Anatomy.

6

GEORGE LAMB

We all want to kiss this Big Brother's Big Mouth.

**You can be
the Sheriff of
my forest any time.**

Age and maturity have taught Amitabh many things, but he still can't drink milk without spilling it all over his beard.

BENICIO DEL TORO

He's no stranger to Sin City, but we still would.

Cary and Audrey's two-person coat made walking surprisingly difficult.

Christopher was never very good at hiding surprises.

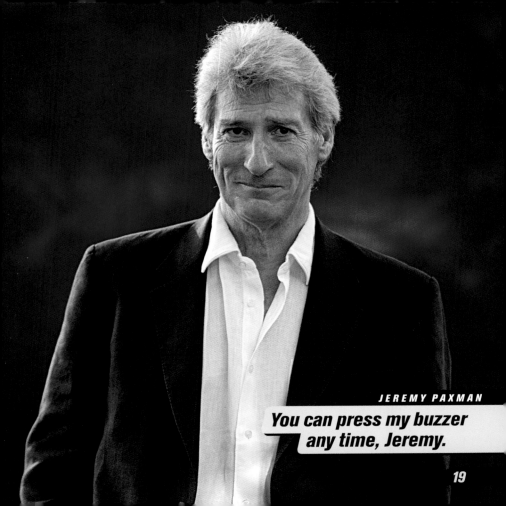

JEREMY PAXMAN

You can press my buzzer
any time, Jeremy.

19

CLINT EASTWOOD

Oh Clint, I know a bunch of girls who would love to go ahead and make your day.

21

DAN LOBB

Let's face it, there are not many other reasons to watch Daybreak.

DAVID ESSEX

The only way is Essex.

'Because I'm worth it.'

Phillip's dandruff was starting to cause a real problem on the set of This Morning.

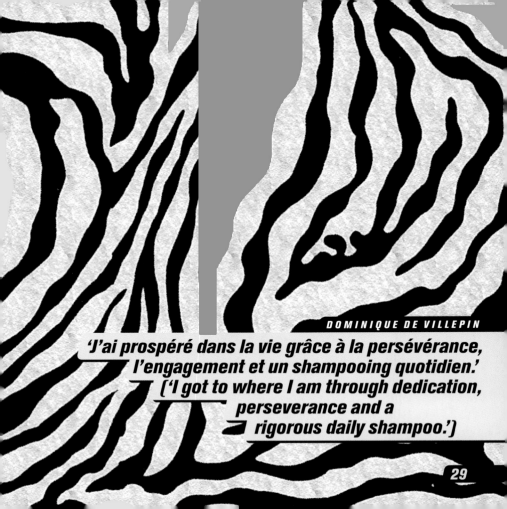

DOMINIQUE DE VILLEPIN

'J'ai prospéré dans la vie grâce à la persévérance,
l'engagement et un shampooing quotidien.'
('I got to where I am through dedication,
perseverance and a
rigorous daily shampoo.')

29

'Put that camera down
and kiss me.'

George was up in the air as to which Nespresso pod to have that morning.

How much for the entire night, Richard? I'll pay anything!

The naked lady to the left of Hugh got exactly the reaction she was looking for.

Too old to be sexy?
What a load of Schmidt!

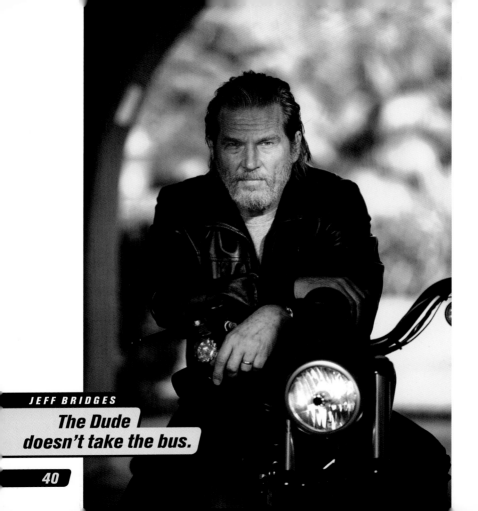

JEFF BRIDGES

***The Dude
doesn't take the bus.***

40

JEFF GOLDBLUM

Looking pretty fly, Jeff.

41

JOHN THAW

**Please sir,
can I have some Morse?**

45

JON SNOW

'It's true what they say,
newsreaders are casual
from the waist down.
Right now I am wearing tennis shorts
with my socks pulled up.'

46

JON STEWART
Our **Daily Show**
of foxiness.

BURT BACHARACH

Burt was delighted to be named the new face of Ariel Ultra.

49

*José never wanted to be
remembered for his looks,
but more for what he did with his balls.*

Junichiro was first in the Japanese sweepstake to guess the size of Kate and Wills' first baby.

LESLIE NIELSEN

He who smelt it dealt it.

To be fair, going out with Peggy Mitchell would turn anybody grey...

Michael deeply regretted scratching his forehead after messing with the super glue.

MORGAN FREEMAN

He's Morgan sexy.

MARK HARMON

'Right, who is next in line
for an examination?'
'ME. IT'S ME, MARK!'

62

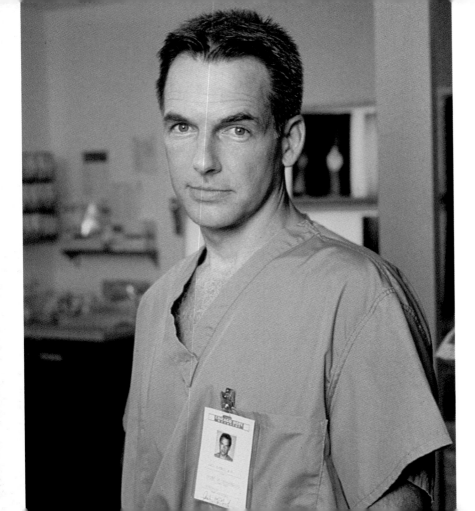

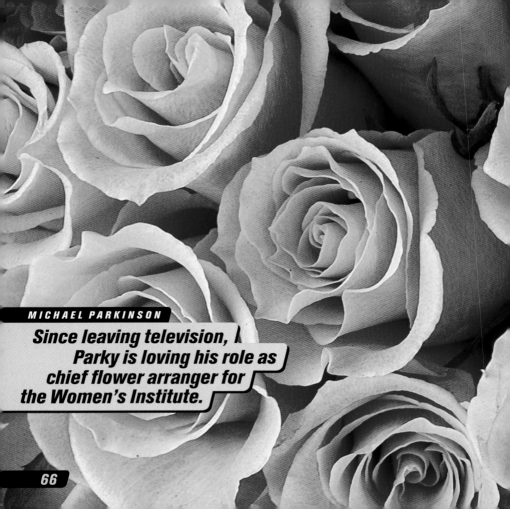

MICHAEL PARKINSON

Since leaving television,
Parky is loving his role as
chief flower arranger for
the Women's Institute.

NIGEL HAVERS

The arch enemy of Peter Pantene.

Omar had a great time at his Bucks Fizz-themed birthday party.

71

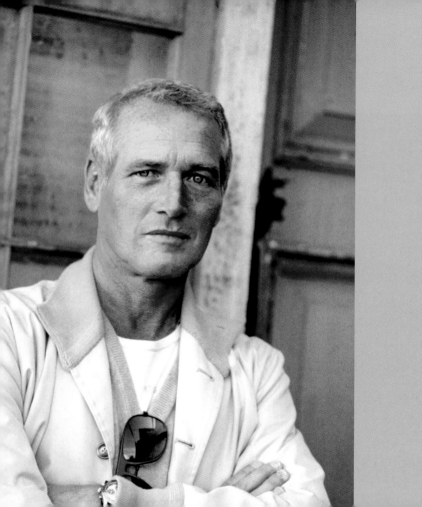

As always, Paul insisted on having his picture taken against a wall that matched his eyes.

Sam was proud of himself for sucking his fruit pastille for so long, but he finally gave in and agreed they really are 'impossible not to chew'.

74

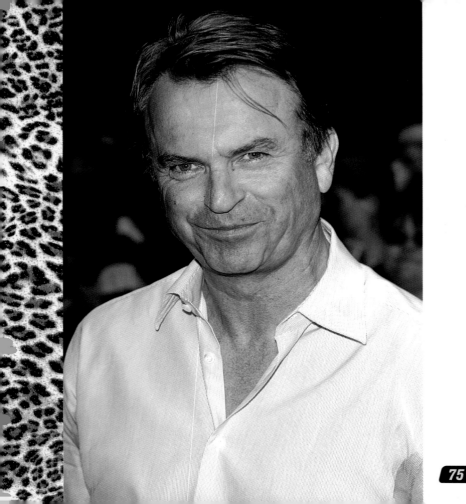

'The hair is brown,
really brown.'
(Sure it is Pierce, sure it is.)

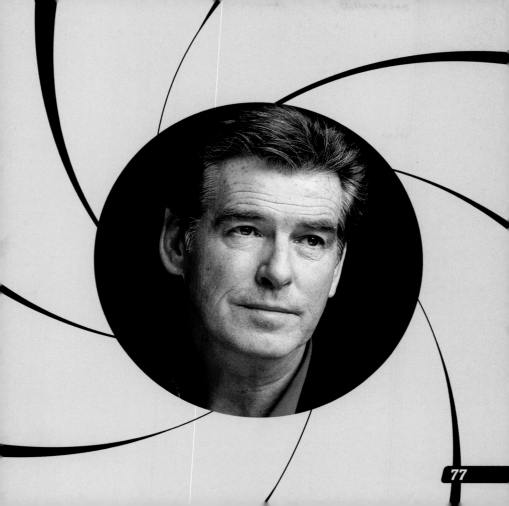

RICHARD E GRANT

Baby's got blue eyes.

78

SEAN CONNERY

We would never say never to you, Sean.

HARRISON FORD

Hair Force One.

80

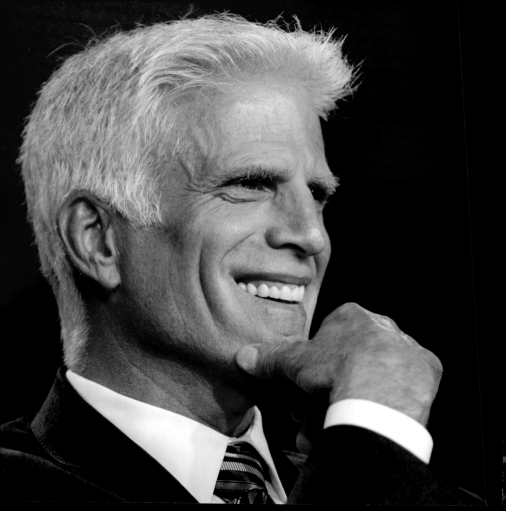

**Ted loved being
a judge at the
Miss World competition.**

Terry was determined to show Ireland that he should represent them at Eurovision, not Jedward.

**You can keep
your hair on.**

And tonight on News at Ten, hundreds of silver foxes have been seen prowling the streets of Central London. Luckily though, I am still the coolest one. Grrrrr. Goodnight.

ALAN DALE

Everybody needs hot neighbours.

90

VIGGO MORTENSEN

Lord of the Ringlets.

Everyone tried to tell Gary that customs would never accept this as his passport photo.

INDEX

PICTURE CREDITS